Marion Public Library
1095 6th Avenue
Marion, IA 52302-3428
(319) 377-3412

A **female** spiny anteater lays an egg and puts it in her pouch. After the puggle hatches, it stays in the pouch for eight weeks.

Spiny anteaters and **platypuses** are the only **mammals** that lay eggs.

Soon the puggle's sharp spines start to grow. The mother digs a **burrow** and leaves the puggle in it.

The mother returns once a week to feed the puggle.

The puggle stays in the **burrow** for about five months. Then it is old enough to find food on its own.

10

Spiny anteaters eat termites, ants, **larvae**, and earthworms. They use their long, sticky tongues to catch their **prey**.

A spiny anteater's mouth is tiny. It's just big enough for the tongue to stick out.

Spiny anteaters look for food by carefully sniffing the forest floor. They can also hear insects moving underground.

Spiny anteaters do not have any teeth.

Spiny anteaters have very strong claws. They can break up logs to find insects.

When a spiny anteater is scared, it digs a hole and hides. Its spines stick out of the ground to **protect** it.

A spiny anteater can also roll into a tight, prickly ball.

Dingoes sometimes hunt spiny anteaters.

Once they are **weaned,** spiny anteaters live alone. They only spend time together during **mating season.**

Another name for spiny anteater is *echidna* (i-KID-na).

Fun Fact
About the Spiny Anteater

A spiny anteater's tongue is 6 inches (15 cm) long. That's about the same length as a hot dog!

6 inches (15 cm)

23

Glossary

burrow – a hole or tunnel dug in the ground by a small animal for use as shelter.

dingo – an Australian wild dog.

female – being of the sex that can produce eggs or give birth. Mothers are female.

larva – a newly hatched wingless insect, before it transforms.

mammal – a warm-blooded animal that has hair and whose females produce milk to feed their young.

mating season – the time of year when male and female animals mate.

platypus – a mammal with webbed feet and a wide bill that lives on the coast of Australia.

prey – an animal that is hunted or caught for food.

protect – to guard someone or something from harm or danger.

weaned – no longer getting milk from one's mother.

To see a complete list of SandCastle™ books and other nonfiction titles from ABDO Publishing Company, visit **www.abdopublishing.com**.

8000 West 78th Street, Edina, MN 55439

800-800-1312 • 952-831-1632 fax